MAGNITUDE OF WHISPERS

MAGNITUDE OF WHISPERS

LISTENING WITH THE HEART
TO TIMELESS TRUTHS

NITA RATHBUN

Library of Congress Control Number: 2020907926
ISBN: Hardcover   978-1-9845-7781-8
                 Softcover   978-1-9845-7780-1
                 eBook   978-1-9845-7777-1

Scripture quotations marked KJV are from the Holy Bible, King James Version (Authorized Version). First published in 1611. Quoted from the KJV Classic Reference Bible, Copyright © 1983 by The Zondervan Corporation.

Scripture quotations marked NIV are taken from the Holy Bible, New International Version®. NIV®. Copyright © 1973, 1978, 1984 by International Bible Society. Used by permission of Zondervan. All rights reserved. [Biblica]

Print information available on the last page.

Rev. date: 04/30/2020

To order additional copies of this book, contact:
Xlibris
1-888-795-4274
www.Xlibris.com
Orders@Xlibris.com
811571

ABOUT THE AUTHOR

Nita Rathbun, for over twenty years, was manager of an insurance company, and later became director of a large medical practice. Aware of the critical nature of listening, she stressed that value to her employees.

As a child, Nita was moved from the small dairy farms of Sulfur Springs to Garland, near Dallas, and saw hippies seek wisdom from Ouija boards, swinging pendulums, and crystals. Later with kids, she hungered to remember the voices of comfort she'd heard in her mind and began writing those words.

Now, after recording those words for more than fifty years, Nita feels moved to share those communications from a larger consciousness with others, as witness to what she intuitively feels are timeless truths. And as the words of a prayer are precious, she hopes that spiritual growth will be stimulated in those who listen with their hearts

INTRODUCTION

The first thing that I would like to tell you is, I am not unique. I am not a psychic or mystic. I do not foretell the specific future. The only thing that makes me different from any one of you is that I am open to the possibility of a universal conscience. I will not name this. I do not believe that this knowledge has to have a name or explanation. When I posed this question of "Who are you?" in my mind. I received this.

"We are here and we will always be here, here in every fiber of your being. Do not fret about the who or where. Truth is truth; that is all that is important. You are not unique in the sense that everyone, or anyone, can or could tap into this universal conscience or thought. This has been done for centuries. This is not magic, but the power and ability in each of you, the problem is that the belief system in your society closes the connection. You believe that it is wrong to hear voices. However, each of you hear them every day. They tell you what is good and what is evil. The problem is when you do hear and chose to listen or heed these voices. Because you have chosen to listen and write down these thoughts given to you, you are afraid that you will be labeled as strange. What is strange is that the voices have been there since the day that you were born and that you stopped listening. There have been in your life and in everyone's lives that the day-to-day task of just living has quieted the voices of the multitude. You only make life more difficult. Why, if help and understanding are as close to you as your heart, do you choose to shut the knowledge out? The soul and along with it the knowledge held by that soul live on. This knowledge from so many surrounds each of you. You have a choice as to which channel you listen to any given minute. They are all the truth, and all truth is good. The evil or bad is created in your own mind. Yes, there is evil and bad in this world. Where does it come from? You know that evil breeds evil. You do not have to choose to listen to mankind or that evil that is in mankind. You will always know what the truth is. Everyone is blessed with an internal thermometer that tells us. This is truth. This is good. When we feel this, then we should listen with our heart and should take heed. When we feel the internal tick that this does not feel like truth, reject it and turn away from it."

We are truth. Go in truth.

I am a clairaudient.

My grandmother was highly sensitive. She was a healer and believed in the importance of dreams. She started the Church of God in Garland, Texas. I grew up with the knowing that God was always with us.

Without knowing what the ability to hear voices was, I kept this ability hidden. This ability developed in my twenties. So for over fifty years, I have heard the voices from above guiding me in writing what I hear. I did not know the name of this ability, only that I was told to write. Sometimes this comes as poetry, however, mostly as wisdom writings. I write what I hear with my inner ear. I do not interpret this. I believe that each one who reads these writings will receive their own message. Each message starts with "We are here." In some of these messages, they explain who the "We" is.

Go in peace and know that God is here to guide, educate, and direct you.

We are here, and you have opened your mind to the things that are important for you to hear. "The times they are a changing." This quote is so true at this time. You are seeing this every day. The changes are happening rapidly. Do not be afraid. Not all the changes are bad. The world had to change. It could not go on as it was. The greed was causing the hearts of men to become void of compassion and caring for their fellow man. The events of these times have changed that. The sacrifice of a relatively few has changed a nation. These souls were meant for this event. They knew that this was their life's mission. Feel sorrow for the world, not for the souls that are, of course, in a better place than the small planet. They have now seen the universe. The war of good and evil will continue. We will tell you this again and again. You will see evil daily until the war focuses on evil, not a place or person. Evil can be seen in the person you are looking at. The small evil flame may flicker in the one standing next to you. The only way to extinguish that evil is with good. This sounds trite but is true. Do good and love one another. Help people without having to have a horrible event happen. Give to those in need. Send love to the unlovable, because only then will there be no need for catastrophes. We know that this concept is a hard one to grasp; however, grasp it you and the world must. Otherwise the destruction will continue. We have told you that this was not for punishment. This was for the love of mankind. There will be other souls sacrificed. Do not be dismayed. This is a choice made before they began this life. Things do not just happen. Your soul has a plan. You are not just plopped down to live out your life and jerked back when it ends. Why would a God that made heaven and earth have such a small scope as to put mankind in that small time frame? Look at the big picture. Know that everything happens for a reason in God's own time and for his purpose.

Go in peace and understanding.

We are here as always.

Do not fear, however, do prepare. Not with food and drink, but prepare your soul. Would you not want to meet the "most important" person in your lifetime with clean hands? Then why would you not want to meet your God with a clean soul? Pray often and tell those around you to prepare with prayers of love and peace.

Go in love

We are here in the light and love of your soul. You are truly enlightened and you should spread that light to the world. Sometimes it is hard for you to put in words your knowing. Do not be dismayed. If you are giving truths, they will someday understand. When the time is right for the soul to understand, no matter the messenger, or what the form of the truths, they will understand. We are always here to help you form the words. Take time to write and do not be afraid or hesitant to speak the truth. Your mate is enlightened but has not formed his core belief. You can help with the knowing.

Go in love and light up your world

We are here. Do not forget to write. That is what is most important. Your putting your writings in order to give the word to other people is also important, but do not put this above listening to our truths.

We know that there is dying and hurting in your world today. Pray for the survivors. Those that you have learned did not survive are thriving in heaven. Each has been welcomed into the loving arms. There is no one reason that this happened except evil. Evil is alive and thriving in your world. The only thing that can eradicate this is goodness. No amount of money or medicine can take the evil from somebody. They were not born evil, but it was instilled in them. This may have come from abuse, poverty, neglect, medication, drugs, or from the evil imparted by other people. However, this evil was put in them. It destroyed the speck of goodness in their soul, and replaced it with hate and the despise of their self. They will be given a chance to forgive themselves and others. However, it may take many lifetimes and many learning experiences for this to happen. God is forgiveness. He holds no hate but is a teacher of love and kindness. As with a child, they need to learn the rules. They will be taught and led to become a more enlightened soul. They may have to endure many painful lifetimes in order to attain this. It takes so little to lead a lifetime of love and service to others. Teach this to all you touch. This life is just a drop in the eternity of your forever. Do not waste it. Teach them, preach to them, love them, and heal all those you touch. The most important minutes of your life should be filled with these actions.

We are here and welcome you. We know that you have a question about hearing from one or many. Sometimes one step forward, but most times it is the collective souls that advise you. Your friends and family are part of that large group. Each adds to the knowledge that we impart to you. If you have a specific soul that you think would give you knowledge or understanding, we can ask that soul for advice to pass to you. You have many who care greatly about you and your well-being. It was difficult for two of those to come to you. It took great energy for them to show themselves to you. They came to show you that souls never die; they just pass to a different realm. They love you and always will. They came to show you that love is eternal and that they will always be at your side. Now to your new adventure. You have always had the ability to heal. We all have it, but do not know how to channel it. We are proud you are learning this. Do not do this for money or to show someone that you are better. Just use it to heal and pray for that person. Don't let your ego get in front of you. Keep humble and help those who need your help. You were put on this earth for a purpose, and part of that was healing. You have a good heart and love to give.

Go in peace and light.

We are here in your heart and caring for your soul. Do not fret about people not having enough of your writings. You can write and hear our teachings anytime you choose to do so. Let your focus be on the hearing and write! This is so simple, but so few do this. We will teach you each time you write. We would like to convey to you the importance of the souls on earth today, learning that they can elevate their souls and go to heaven, even if there are things that they have done on earth that would deter them in the straight path to heaven. Start now. Learn how to live with God at the center of your world. You do not have to be inside a church to pray and study his word. Learn what was said about good and evil. Being lax in learning is as bad as sinning. You have to learn the truths. How do you know how to react to the people you meet? How do know how to forgive those who have hurt you? How do you know what is the truth or what is false? Read, study, and ask questions of those who do know.

Go in peace and learn the way.

We are here. We know that you are wondering what the future may hold. No need to wonder. It will hold love and laughter, joy and sadness. You will have times of peace and times of turmoil. It has always been so and will always been so.

Relationships: Do not go into a relationship to change them. No one ever really changes. If you see things you do not like, that will not change. Whether it be clothes in the middle of the floor or ideas. Ask yourself if these things are important to you. If they are important, then they will always be a thorn in your side. However, if the heart of a person is more important than the outward mess, then you are the one who has to change your ideas of what is important. You can pick up the mess and go on, but you can't put things in a person's soul that are not there. Do not let your past get caught up in your future. Do not rerun old movies. Go forward with a clean slate and write a new beautiful relationship.

We are always with you. You know that we will guide you if you let us. Sometimes you shut us out. Nothing is a sure thing and sometimes we have to venture to gain.

We are here and hear your thoughts. You have asked the question as to why God lets bad things happen to good people. God allows each of us to have free will. Our lives are mapped out in a broad sense as to what we want to achieve in this lifetime. We are also allowed to have the choice as to how we achieve those goals. When other souls interact with us, the way we achieve them may change. We may be given different opportunities and different circumstances to be able to achieve those same goals. If our goal in this life is to learn compassion, there may come one into our life that needs our compassion, but rejects it when we offer it. The timing may be wrong. However, in the rejection we may learn perseverance and achieve another of our goals. God doesn't rule; he guides, as a great teacher would give you guides to learn from. The lessons that we take from this will vary. Do not be dismayed because bad things happen. Those that you perceive as bad for one may not be bad for all. Learning of life's lessons takes many forms. Remember to keep your eyes on the big picture and do not dwell on the small things that distract from your ultimate goal of being one with God. The only way for you to learn life's true lesson is by living each day with this ultimate goal. Ask each day if today you have advanced along that road toward your ultimate destination.

Go in peace and learn to love.

We are here in this space at this time. Be at peace. The time is right for you to begin your writing again. Your focus has been on moving your focus to a new life. That is as it should be. You have found someone who will not only understand your writing but embrace your thoughts and ideas. We are always as near as your next thought if you have the patience to listen to what we tell. Your world may never see peace, but the time will come when some of the turmoil in some of your world will lessen. However, it will surface again in other parts.

Your world is not willing to do without wars for to change would mean that all would have to accept the ideas of others as valid. Not only religion of all people, but the inner core belief of others. Not only the way in which they worship their God. But accept that their God is your God. Your world is not ready to accept that—so you will have war over this acceptance. You may change your place in the world when you and you alone accept this principle. Then your own world, the realm that you may reach, may be changed.

Go in peace and change your inner belief and change your world.

We are here. Do not be afraid of "end times." There is no such thing as the end. Even if you die, that is not the end of your soul. So why would you worry about everyone saying you are in the end of times. Does it mean that it is the time to see God and have him see you? You already do that. The end times will mean the end of evil and all the bad. Does that sound like something you should dread? No, it will be a time of rejoicing, a "jubilee," or a time of happiness.

You will be with those who crossed over—all those that have died for you and those that you have been with in many past lives.

Go in peace and do not fear the future.

We are here to guide you into the knowledge of the ages and acknowledge it is truth. There is much turmoil on this planet at this time. This too will pass. There is peace in the heavenly realm and that is what matters. You have the inner knowledge about Jesus and his sacrifice to save not only your world but all worlds. He is not only called God's son, but is an actual piece of the Godhead. His presence on earth was planned as a way to show all what pure love is. It is still the same. The worship by many religions, which go by many names, all have the same "Godhead" to show what love is. The teaching should only be that they emulate that love and show it to each of you. No matter how unlovable some of those are. Love changes not only those that you show it to but changes those that show it. Your soul is elevated and your soul enlightened by the giving more than the getting. Especially in giving to those who do not want your love or even your pity. They have built a fence of anger and hate not only for love, but for compassion and giving. When someone realizes how much destructing they have caused to others, then they wall themselves in a self-imposed cage where only hate can get in. They will have many lessons to learn when they pass from this world. There is never hate in heaven. There is only truth and knowledge. Showing love for all is not easy, in fact it is extremely difficult. Opening your eyes to the truth is like taking off dark glasses, and seeing the sunshine for the first time. It hurts your eyes and you see too much. You want to return to the safety of those dark glasses. For those that take their time and start looking for the truth, then the world opens up to them. They see colors and shapes they haven't seen before. They become open to new concepts and are truly enlightened.

Go in love and light.

We are here. We haven't left. We understand that you have questions about a past life or lives. Yes, you and everyone living has had a past life. The one you are living now is the most important one. You are using things from those lives. Things that you had to learn to advance. One of those lives was a healer. You are carrying on that attribute. In one life you were treated badly and were of a low class that was tortured and beaten. In that life you had no stature. That is why you feel that you have to prove yourself and be better than I. That is okay if you do not lose sight of your self-worth.

We understand and will guide you to keep this trait in hand. Just remember to keep humble when you impart knowledge or healing. Remember it is not about you. It is about God working through you. Give him the glory and then you will be a true healer.

Go in the light of God's love.

We are here and will always be ready to tell you the truth.

We have heard the earth's prayer for peace. There will eventually be a peace. It may not look like the bucolic peace you want. There will be new people in high places. Some from this world, some from others but more advanced.

God is the ruler over all. That will never change! He is dismayed at the hate that has poisoned this world. He is angry at the hurt the children have suffered. The injustice makes him so sad. It would be simple for him to wipe out this world and begin anew. However, that would not give those alive today the chance to make changes. This helps your world and elevates the souls of those who make those changes. There will be battles, but they will be between good and evil, not countries. This is not going to happen overnight.

It took eons for your world to get to this point, and it will take lifetimes for change to come. There are still those that live on the evil and hate in their hearts. God is the only one that can erase that. Each of you can help by turning away from the evil and showing them the way of love. They will either take this love or reject it. If rejected, then they suffer.

Go in peace and pray for love for all.

We are here as always. You are on the right path. However, you always give up easily. Follow through with your thoughts and prayers. Never stop with following your beliefs. You can change yourself, and by changing you will see a change in others. Do not hesitate to call on your guides. We are the ultimate teachers. Reading is good, but listen to those who truly know it all. Go with your inner thoughts whatever they be about, furniture, or the future.

Be at peace.

We are here in your heart and mind.

Do not be afraid of the future—not this month, year, or decade. We are always here. God doesn't take vacations. He is with you always. Quiet your mind and hear us. The problems that you are listening to are nothing but people trying to increase fear in the world. They will say they know the answers to those fears. Then they will control and help you. They lie. Help yourself with knowledge and prayers for the world. Don't be afraid. What will happen will happen. You can't stop it, but you can stop the way you react to it. You have many angels protecting the people of the planet. Be at peace and pray for peace.

Go in peace and the light of God.

We are here and we understand your fears. You know that the times are very worrying for many. War is not an absolute outcome if the people of earth would just stop and contemplate the consequences for a minute. What are they going to gain except heartbreak and sorrow? Their souls will lose any progress they made in previous lifetimes, and those who come after them will also pay for the wrongs they commit. The ones who have the duty forced on them by people in power will have soul damage as well as damage to their mind and body. This will last until they can repair it in the next life. Your country could be a land of cripples unless the Lord gives the knowledge and power to the wise ones to stop the march to sorrow and pain. Listen carefully to those who have Jesus in their hearts. Show love to their fellow man. There are some with this knowledge of the insight of a possible future, whether from this world or another one. They can make a difference.

Do not be surprised if you hear the voices come to your people shortly. There are wise people that do not like what is happening but are waiting for the people to wake up from the sleep of complacency and realize that the ones who profess to be doing good for all is doing evil for everyone. Any good that is done is coming from those whose love for people is stronger than their love of self. Prayer and inner searching is important at this time.

Love one another and pray for peace, inner and outer.

We are here, and we are glad that you have taken the time to listen to the things that you need to hear. We are pleased that we feel that your country will not be destroyed by war at this time. There will always be people who will not agree. This has been going on since time began. This will continue until time ends and peace comes or until the planet you call home is no longer livable. Because people do not really listen or read about God and his peace, you continue to cause discord in your world. You love those you are close to and hate those whose ideas clash with yours. There are many groups of people that are aligned with a group they call religion. However, their God may be money or power, or a manmade God. Those religions will not last, because there is only one God, and he has nothing to do with those things. Religion has to start in your heart. You have to learn to listen to the still small voice first. Then read and study his teachings. Go to church not for fun, but to truly worship him. This does not mean that you can't worship with praise and shouts. What it does mean is that Christ has to be at the center, and you have to feel his presence no matter what. Go because this is God's house and you are closer to him there than anywhere. Carry him in your heart and soul every day.

Go in his love and seek him always.

Be at peace. Your health is better. Do not think it is bad. There are many that are much worse. You will find your life's journey or destination. Pray about this every day. You have already helped many. You will help many more. Have faith and believe this. Remember to believe and trust in God. That is faith. We gave you the words to say to the church. Now dwell on those words and take them into your heart. You have a helpmate that will help. He is a good and honest man and loves you completely just as you are. He was meant to come into your life and make you a better person. Faith will make you whole.

Go be at peace.

We are here to guide you. You have not been diligent in settling down and quieting your soul. Do not fear. Put that out of your mind. You do not know or have you ever had a reason to fear. Yes, your earth will change, just as it has always changed. Nothing on earth or the universe stays the same. Be ready for change, but do not fear that change. We all change. Life to death to life again. Is that bad? No, it is life. Those you love have gone will come again in time. However, that happens to all. There is bliss when they arrive, and there is a learning period and review of their life between their returns. They have choices to make, just as you have choices in this life to make. You and Larry have made the decision to help people. This is a hard choice, but an applauded one. Do what you can. However, ask for protection and discernment in the help that you give and the choice of who you help. This adventure can help hurt you. You do have to help with things. Help with love. That is an easy thing to give, but sometimes not so easy to accept.

Go in peace and give love every chance you get.

We are here beside you. You have been one of the chosen to say to the world the words of peace and harmony are not coming to an end, but are, in fact, just beginning. Do not listen to those who preach disharmony and use scare tactics to drive people to the church, but teach that the church is for those who listen to the truth in the Bible. We are all created by the same Father, God.

Why then can we not act like we are all brothers and sisters? No matter the color or language, we have the same Father in heaven. It is so wrong to hate your brothers or sisters. It just brings hate back to you when you sling it at someone. In the end of your world, which is very, very far off, you will be as one. Do you want to have alienated those to the point that no one is on that tiny ball but those who killed those who could have helped rebuild a new world?

Love all mankind—red, yellow, black, or white—and make them your allies, not your enemy. This is the only way that your world, and all those on it, will survive. Join hands in holding on to what this world is now, and make it better, not destroyed. Then you can live on it in the future.

Go in peace and join with each of those you touch.

We are here and hearing. We understand you questioning your hearing. We give many gifts to a few people. You have explored your gift of writing. Now explore your other gifts. They all are part of one knowing. Remember to be prudent and prayerful in your spreading of these gifts. You were given them to help and enlighten others. God-given talents are not to be wasted on stunts. Take them like a precious pearl. Do not spread pearls before swine. If you do not trust the person with your knowledge, then do not give it. The gifts we give you are to be used wisely or they will go away. These are not cheap tricks like circus mystics. These are prophetic utterances to be given for growth and enlightenment to you and those that you give them to. These utterances should appease their worries and leave them in a peaceful state. Give them time to reflect on the truth and what to do with the knowledge they gain from it.

Go in peace and disclose with prudence.

We are here. The time to write is always correct. There is no right or wrong. We are always as close as your breath. Do not worry about the things of this world. The world is either in upheaval, or war, or peace. Most of those who inhabit this world are either upset about what is happening in their family, or how much money they don't have, or finding a new job, house, or car. They worry so little about taking care of their soul. A soul is a wondrous thing. You can feed it as you do your body. Feed it with the Word, which tells you how to take care of your soul. It tells you to feed your soul by helping other people feed their soul.

Everyone can be a teacher, preacher, and physician. Teach others to use their talents to elevate the talents of others. God was all of those, and is all of them. So should you be all of those when you preach and teach and heal. God freely gives these talents so that all would be used for his glory. Listen carefully to all he tells you. Everyone has the ability, but is afraid to acknowledge it. Remember all things are sent by God. God does not want pain or hurt for anyone. All they have to do is read and study the Bible—God's how-to book. It is all there. Be a servant to all who need your knowledge or help.

Go into the world and spread the Good News: that God is always with us. He has never gone away.

We are here as always. Quiet your mind and heart and listen. The questions that you pose about the afterlife are asked by everyone. They have been asked for eons. Do not be dismayed because the quick answer is not there. The life after is as sacred as the life before death.

As not each of you accomplish your goals or obtain your success, such as it is in what you call heaven. Our souls achieve goals and have failures. The soul sets these goals for enlightenment and elevation. Few achieve perfection. The process can be completed here or can be supplemented with visits to other growing opportunities. Each soul is given every opportunity needed to obtain perfection. As you said in the writing: "The treasure is the quest." Each soul has eternity to achieve the perfection goal. You have a question as to why we see or dream of souls as we knew them if they are no longer in the body. This is only for those left behind. Would you recognize a spirit? These bodies are not needed by the enlightened, only by those who have to be shown the vessel.

Go in peace and rejoice in your learning.

We are here. Do not be dismayed with the lack of understanding of the gift that you have been given. We understand. That is the most important thing. As it says in the Bible, this is a gift. Why would a gift not be understood? Because if anyone acts in a way that is different than the norm, then it is shunned. Just rejoice in your gift and share the knowledge that we impart. We impart only goodness and truth. Each soul has this knowledge inside. When we die, we are free to impart it. While living, people do not accept it. Then it is thought of as bunk. Knowledge and understanding of the goodness and love of all mankind is not popular. If accepted, then you would have to love all mankind. That will not happen at this time.

Go in peace and love all.

We are here as always. The sharing has begun. You have to start with one. The next telling of our story will be easier. The lessons we are imparting are so important for your world to hear that you mustn't be afraid of the way you are perceived, only the way the message is perceived. This is a time of division in your world, the division of good and evil. Those that are doing evil are doing it in the name of their God. They are saying this with their mouth but are not saying it with their heart. In that place they know that the destruction is not of their God. However, the destruction is truly of your God. A loving God that wants his people to realize that in order to have a blissful eternity, they must focus on it now. The light that shines in each of you needs nurturing. The way to bliss is through this light. Light stands for goodness. You know that white light when broken down is made of many colors. As this is so, know that the light that shines in each of you is many faceted also. There is the light of love for mankind, the light of compassion, the light of knowledge, and the light of generosity. All of these, and many more, together make up your inner light. You can only shine in heaven when all facets are polished on earth. Do not fail in any area. Remember also that you are polished by the rough cloth of adversity. An easy life without trials does nothing to elevate your soul.

Go in the light of love.

We are here, however, the messages are so important that your mind should be focused entirely on them. So quiet your mind first. The message today is the same as it has been since time began. The message is so simple, only man can make it complicated. The reason for man's being is not in this moment; it is not in this lifetime. This lifetime is like a grain of sand in the ocean of time. Is that grain the one that becomes the beach? No, but without it there would be no beach. Be mindful of this lifetime. Enjoy the day, enjoy the minute, but know that each word and deed reflects on your eternity. There is not one sentence written in your book of life that is unimportant. From the day that you are born until the day that this earthly existence ends, each second is recorded. That is why we have told you to live your life like an open book, for it will be open and reviewed for your soul to evaluate. If you thought that someone would examine each of your thoughts and deeds, would you live your life differently? We hope so. This concept has been known for eons, but man has chosen to ignore it and focus on the now. Be the best you can be and elevate your own soul and those that you touch.

Go in peace and tell the world your truths.

We are here in this time and at this place. We realize the concept of a truth that is true and would never be questioned by someone will never happen. Each truth will be rejected by many and accepted by some. When we reveal a truth to you——tell your truth——that is all that we ask. Turn this over to the ones who will hear or read these words. Some will feel the truth in their souls and in the feeling will believe. Some will reject these truths, not because they are not true, but because of their lack of knowledge about these truths. The time is just not correct for them to accept them. They may not accept them in this lifetime, but accept them they will someday. These truths do not go against any beliefs. All beliefs have at their center a higher power. That is the ultimate truth. We are just telling the truth of this higher power. We tell you again that all souls and all beings were allowed to be in this realm for one reason only——to elevate or educate their soul. The only way this can be done is by perfecting it with learning lessons. These lessons can be about love of their fellowman, humility, compassion, joy, and sharing. All of these and many more are attributes of a perfected soul. Each has to be learned and practiced if not in this experience then in the next. This is why some ones seem at peace at the beginning of their life and continue this peace while others are troubled. Some have learned some of the lessons while others have resisted this learning, making them troubled. Each soul is like a piece of clay; each experience molds that soul. Sometimes the free will choice of that soul destroys part of that which has been created. This causes that soul to have the part molded again.

Go in love and learn . . .

We are here. Do not be dismayed about your lack of understanding about the concept of souls sacrificing for the good of mankind. You have to understand that this is not the first time; this is usually the case when there is a war. The conscience of a nation is always changed. Go back through history and examine the times of a great change in conscience or thinking. These changes were proceeded by a catastrophe, usually war or at the least a large number of deaths in something that related to a banding together for change. The Holocaust and the persecution of Christians all were souls sacrificed for change. Each of these souls came to this existence for that purpose. The reason that knowledge is not available to the entity before the event is evident. They would not understand. In a few of the cases, these souls had a feeling in their heart that they were here for a larger purpose. The majority of the firemen and policemen knew that they were driven to help mankind, otherwise they would not have chosen those professions. We leave this place you call heaven with a purpose and an opportunity to elevate our souls. Some succeed. Some fail, however, all are given the opportunity for success. The ones who choose to set up roadblocks by choosing evil or deception are losing the "chance of a lifetime" literally.

Go in peace and pray for understanding.

We are here, and this is a good time for openness. We will try to educate you in our ways. However, do not be dismayed if your message is not well received by many. It is very hard for people to believe that their existence is for one purpose and one purpose only. That purpose is to elevate their soul. What other purpose do they think is more important? Do they think that the accumulation of wealth and power is going to be carried with them in the hereafter? How would that be possible? The one who is poor and has struggled but retained his dignity and elevated those he has come in contact with will be the one that has stepped a rung higher on the ladder to a more elevated eternity. The beggar on the street who feels sorry for his position and is bitter about society and sees no good in this world will stay as he is. However, the penniless who can rejoice in a sunset or see the joy in a child's smile will step higher. Money is not a measure of wealth. Goodness and the ability to show the world this goodness and the willingness to fight against evil is a measure of wealth and not only wealth, eternal wealth. We would like to proclaim. Go forth. Spread joy. Spread goodness. See beauty and spread the truth in your deeds and in your words.

Go into the world with truth.

We are here when the time is quiet and your mind is at peace. Do not be troubled by the difficulty some have in understanding your message. Those that need to know the truth will seek the truth. You cannot force others to drink of the river of knowledge. They will come to have this thirst someday, if not in this lifetime or this realm, in another. You can only offer this bread that will cure all hunger. Some will go hungry. Do what you can to spread the simple message that this lifetime counts for an eternity, that each moment is important and that no one should waste the precious small amount of time that they are given. You are a teacher and you will always be a guide in this realm and other realms. This has been so in the past, present, and will be so in the future. Gird yourself for this task and take back to the other lives as much knowledge and understanding, not only of yourself, but of others, as you can carry.

Go in love and guide with patience.

We are here. You will someday understand the we. We know that you have many questions on the why. This would be revealed now if it were necessary. Just focus on the goal. Do not question the messengers of truth and enlightenment. Knowledge is not something that is given unless there is a reason for that knowledge. Even though we hold all knowledge, we give on the sustenance that is needed for the soul. You need only know what truth is. We give you the truths for you to tell others. That is the message and will always be the message. The messengers will vary as they are needed. You need not know the messengers. Some you have known on this and other realms. Some are only guides and have never been on your plain. All are elevated souls or they would not be allowed to teach. Teaching truths is a very elevated position. Few are chosen for this. The guides that are your teachers are old souls who have guided many.

Go in peace and understanding

We are here. Be at peace. Do not be afraid to venture into the unknown. If you never step out in faith that God will guide you, you will never be able to walk in his light. The times are troubling, but there is a reason. People have to start focusing on the things that are truly important, and not on the worldly things that they strive so hard for. When their focus becomes their eternal soul and how to become the best that they can be on earth in order to gain grace in heaven, then the focus will change. God does not punish his people. The devil uses people for his purpose. This includes using their fear. Do not be fearful of what is happening on earth. Be fearful of what could happen in heaven. Live your life like an open book, loving all mankind. You do not need someone else to be fulfilled. You need to stay focused on you and what your eternal needs will be instead of trying to fulfill everyone else's needs on earth. Your family and friends can do for themselves if you will let go. Stay concerned, but let the reins loose. Only then can you all focus on your own needs for the future. We will not reveal your future—no one should.

You will live it one day at a time. Be the best that you can be in the moment, and the future will unfold one moment at a time. The day should begin and end with a prayer. Pray for peace. Pray for the overcoming of evil. Pray for the souls of all those who have been destroyed by evil, whether they be victims or perpetrators. Evil did destroy them. The evil in this world is strong, but good and God are stronger. Clutch that good and use it for the betterment of all you touch. Only you can use your talents to reach those you come in contact with.

Go in peace.

We are here, and you have opened your mind to the things that are important for you to hear. "The times they are a changing." This quote is so true at this time. You are seeing this every day. The changes are happening rapidly. Do not be afraid. Not all the changes are bad. The world had to change. It could not go on as it was. The greed was causing the hearts of men to become void of compassion and caring for their fellow man. The events of these times have changed that. The sacrifice of a relatively few has changed a nation. These souls were meant for this event. They knew that this was their life's mission. Feel sorrow, for the world, not for the souls that are, of course, in a better place than the small planet. They have now seen the universe. The war of good and evil will continue. We will tell you this again and again. You will see evil daily until the war focuses on evil, not a place or person. Evil can be seen in the person you are looking at. The small evil flame may flicker in the one standing next to you. The only way to extinguish that evil is with good. This sounds trite but is true. Do good and love one another. Help people without having to have a horrible event happen. Give to those in need. Send love to the unlovable, because only then will there be no need for catastrophes. We know that this concept is a hard one to grasp, however, grasp it you and the world must. Otherwise the destruction will continue. We have told you that this was not for punishment. This was for the love of mankind. There will be other souls sacrificed. Do not be dismayed. This is a choice made before they began this life. Things do not just happen. Your soul has a plan. You are not just plopped down to live out your life and jerked back when it ends. Why would a God that made heaven and earth have such a small scope as to put mankind in that small time frame? Look at the big picture. Know that everything happens for a reason in God's own time and for his purpose.

Go in peace and understanding.

We are here when you need to tap the universal flow of consciousness. Be still in your heart and in your mind. The day's troubles are causing your focus to be clouded.

Do not fret about the evil of the world. There has to be evil, otherwise there would be all good and no challenges. Then you would be in heaven. The reason for the bad that happens to man is so that they will strive for a better place where there is no bad. Bad things happen to everyone at times in their lives. There is no one who goes through life unscarred by the knives of hurt. When we learn to heal these hurts and defend ourselves against more hurts, then we have elevated our souls. Pray with compassion for those that are hurting in body and in soul. They need prayers, which are alerts for those that love them, on whatever plain, to search for ways to help. Their prayers and yours will be answered. As we have told you, they may not be the answer that you expect, but they will be answered.

Go in love and prayer.

We are here, as you know. We have been with you since birth. We are with everyone. They just are not tuned to the right channel to hear our wisdom. The universal pool of knowledge is here to be tapped into by anyone at any time. It is for you to teach others to learn to listen. Why when all knowledge is available to everyone, those who need it most do not search for it. They choose instead to listen to those who have bits and pieces of the wisdom. All knowledge is available, however, you have to listen with your heart and soul, not only with your mind and ears. This is very difficult for some. They are not open to the idea that this light can shine on them. They are closed to the idea of universal wisdom.

However, they are quick to believe in the wisdom of men on the earth realm that use wisdom created in the time of eyeblinks rather than eternities.

Go in love and understanding and teach the world love.

We are here. We know that your heart and mind are troubled by the events that are taking place at this time. War has been around since the beginning of man. The war that is being fought now is not about land, or even about religion, as wars in the past, but about the evil that has been let loose in this world against the good in men's hearts. This evil is not a man, but the focus has become on this evil one. Yes, he is evil, however, the disease of evil is far more prevalent than one man. Each of us has to fight first the evil and hate in our own hearts before we can fight the evil in another person. You can kill this one, but many will be left in his wake. The evil has to be extinguished one flame at a time and replaced with that flame of goodness that, when allowed to burn in each of us, burns out the evil. We do not know when this battle will end, however, the battle between evil and good will never end. Do not think that this will be over and that your duty will be done. Be vigilant every day to see the evil and wrongdoings. Each one of you must stamp out that flame. Each one of you must fight every day for good, just as diligently as you fight against evil. Heaven is not a place. Heaven is here in your heart. Yes, you will be with God one day, but if you want your eternity to be at his hand, then your deed must be written with your own hand showing that you were willing to stand against the evil one and say, "No more." Write that on your scroll for eternity to see.

Go in peace and live in harmony.

We are here as you know. To call us angels means putting a name to thoughts. Yes there are angels who watch over you. But you do not have to have a shape to be watched by. You are surrounded by a heavenly energy that guides you by thoughts. This is what protects you, not wings. When you can quiet your mind to listen, anyone can hear the voice of the angels. You have become better at it this past year. Your heart has not been as troubled and your mind is at peace. We can come to you anytime you need us. We know that you are in turmoil about your future. You are learning to listen to your soul. It is trying to help you stay strong.

Step out into the future in the faith that we are always with you.

We are here and welcome you. We know that you have a question about hearing from one or many. Sometimes one may step forward, but most times it is the collective souls that advise you. Your friends and family are part of that large group. Each adds to the knowledge that we impart to you. If you have a specific soul that you think would give you knowledge or understanding, we can ask that soul for advice to pass to you. You have many who care greatly about you and your well-being. It was difficult for two of those to come to you. It took great energy for them to show themselves to you. They came to show you that souls never die; they just pass to a different realm. They love you and always will. They came to show you that love is eternal and that they will always be at your side. Now to your new adventure. You have always had the ability to heal. We all have it, but do not know how to channel it. We are proud you are learning this. Do not do this for money or to show someone that you are better. Just use it to heal and pray for that person. Don't let your ego get in front of you. Keep humble and help those who need your help. You were put on this earth for a purpose, and part of that was healing. You have a good heart and love to give.

Go in peace and light.

We are here. Here in your heart and in your hands. We will send you an urgent message today. Not of doom, but of hope. The prayers of many have been sent up since the attack of evil. Never think that the Power is not open to prayer. That is all that has ever been asked of your world—that you be mindful of him. And when you pray to your higher power, you are mindful. This power of prayer is the only thing that *can* change the course of your world. Everyone in all countries uniting in prayer has influenced the course of your world. The goodness is the now. Only those that continue to pray for peace and goodness can continue this change or reprieve of your world. Remember, your world was created for the betterment of each individual soul. If that place does not sustain those souls, then they will move on to another place. For now in this time and in this place, your world is a better world.

Go in peace and harmony.

We are here in your mind and soul. Do not be afraid of the future. Be afraid of not doing the spirit work today. Take the time to practice holiness. Do good and help your fellow man. Then you will have an afterlife not filled with regrets and sorrows about what you should have done. Love those that are close to you and spread that love to all you touch. We know that fear freezes the good deeds that you can do. Do not be afraid of trying to heal. You are not the one who decides to heal someone. God is!

Go in peace in the light of love and walk with God each day.

We are here and the time for prayer and contemplation is now. When you pray, you open the direct channel not only to your higher conscience but to all those who have gone before and will come after. This knowledge of the greater good is laid on a table waiting. Prayer puts your mind in an open state, so therefore be mindful of what you pray for. Do not waste this openness by praying to win the lottery. This is not the purpose of prayer. You can pray for your loved ones, but for their eternal gains, not physical gains. You may pray for peace and understanding and you may pray for guides in your daily life. Those are prayers that will be answered as soon as they are uttered. The minute that you pray for love or the millisecond you pray for higher understanding, the prayer is answered. You have this answered prayer with you so that when the thought is formed, the answer is there. All you need to do is listen.

Go in love and pray for understanding.

We are here, still. You have posed the question about God in many forms in many nations with different religions. There is one Supreme Being—one God. There are many different ways to get to the presence of that God. All religions have this as the goal, although they may call it by different names. There have been many different prophets that have shown their believers different paths to follow to reach the ultimate destination. As on a roadmap, you will see that you can follow many roads. Some will take you longer to reach your intended goal, but all will reach it eventually. This should not be of great concern. If a prophet teaches truths and shows the followers a way to reach this bliss, it doesn't matter that the teachings are in a different tongue. The prophet that teaches untruths only delays the followers in reaching their destination, however, he does not keep them from getting there. Their journey will not be as easy and they may have to retrace their steps, however, they will reach their presence with God. This road will be a little more bumpy and filled with ruts. There are some who are alienated from God for eternity and whose goal is to divert others to their path, however, these true evil ones are few. God is a loving and understanding presence, and his joy is in the reuniting of souls with his light.

Go in love and live in God's light.

We are here. The concept of closeness to the God is not meant to be a closeness in terms of vicinity or distance. It is a closeness of becoming one with the Higher Power. As each soul is perfected, they become more Godlike and become closer to the perfection that is God. This is the soul's goal whether they realize it on this plane or not. When the earthly entity has been dropped, they will be back on target for the soul's goals. You do not have to push this belief as each has it written into their Book of Life. It would be easier if each one knew this and strived for this perfection, however, each soul is on the perfection path.

Go in enlightenment

We are here, one with you. Be at peace and hold space in your heart. The world, or part of your world, is in turmoil at this time. It has always been so. Souls grow from adversity and turmoil. In times of peace and quiet, the opportunity for growth is not as great. It is great for those who are oppressed to learn the lessons of love and forgiveness. And it is great for those who are there to help the oppressed to learn the lessons of love and to learn how to give wholeheartedly to those in need. Those who created the oppression are evil and will have to learn the compassion lesson another time and place. Always remember that things happen just as they are supposed to. Nothing is unexplained in the great plan.

Go in love and peace and pray for those who know no peace.

We are here as always. Listen with your heart and you will know that this is true. Your world is in very turbulent times. When the fighting reaches the holy places, this is a very disturbing time for you. Know that there is a reason for this to be happening at a time when your religion celebrates the birth of one who proclaimed the teachings of God in that place. Wake up to the meaning that when people see that the holiest is not sacred, they should be aware that the world, and ideas that they hold dear, is not sacred, and that evil is out to destroy even what they hold dear. Proclaim that evil should be sought out before it destroys not only your holy sites but your world. Evil holds nothing as sacred—not people or places. The evil that has been let loose in your world will be a stubborn foe. The good that is in the hearts of the righteous is the only thing that can destroy it. The fighting will only destroy a small portion, and some of those who fight enjoy the killing. How can this then be destroying evil? Not with killing. That will only destroy man, not the evil he breeds. Go forth and teach that goodness must thrive and grow in every heart and in every land.

Go in peace and proclaim goodness.

This was a day when I found out that I had a suspicious mammogram.

On my calendar for the day:
Peace I leave with you: my peace I give you. I do not give to you as the world gives. Do not let your hearts be troubled and do not be afraid.

John 14:27 NIV

We are here. We will always be your comfort and your guide. We send you messages in many ways. We will be beside you in any of the trying times as we are in the good times. Keep your heart open to our messages as well as your mind and your eyes. Listen to our knowledge. Your fear is of the unknown. When the unknown becomes known, then you will have something to focus on. Until then be at peace with the knowledge that nothing is overwhelming unless allowed to become so. Each crisis becomes a learning lesson. Do not go forward with fear, only with the understanding that you are not alone and will never be alone even through eternity.

Go with love and our thoughts and knowledge.

We are here. There is no timetable for when you need to put your thoughts on paper. The more you learn and the faster you learn it, the more able you are to spread the truth. Your mission is not an easy one. Truth is not something people want to hear. They want to create their own reality—that their purpose in life is to acquire things and make sure that their children are prepared in life so that they can acquire things. The purpose should be to prepare their children to acquire a more fulfilling eternity. This is done by teaching them truths. The truths that helping your fellowman is helping yourself, that hate and hurt will do you harm as well. This lesson should begin when they are small and their minds are open. It is only when they grow that the connection becomes strained. The young still remember the place they came from. That is why we can see the wonder in their eyes. That is why they have such joy. The parents should build on that joy and learn to see it themselves. Every day should include a lesson—the way to enhance the joy so that it will last a lifetime.

Go in understanding and stand for knowledge.

We are here in your heart and soul. Do not be afraid of new ventures, whether they are jobs or relationships. Only by trying new things do you learn. If none stepped out to see the other side of their small world, there would be no learning. This fear of the other side of the wall holds so many in their box. Try new things on and see if they fit your knowing. If they are not needed, file or discard them, and go on to the next learning experience. This is a scary concept for some who would rather feel safe in the known. However, this leaves no room for growth. Learn new lessons every day. Try new worlds and see new sights. This will add to your knowledge not only in this realm, but also for your eternity.

Go in knowledge and see new sights.

We are here in the guise of guides. We can only guide. We cannot compel. The free will of man is what makes them men. God does not want to force his will. The decisions that each man makes mold the entity for eternity. If God were to force his will, each mold would be the same. Each soul will make many mistakes in a lifetime, with corrections in the next. If these corrections are not made, then the opportunity to make them will again be given. The soul is perfected by this process. There are few who are deemed without flaws. That is the idea that each should hold to the highest goal. That is the meaning of life. That is the reason for life. God could make the corrections and take away the choice, but each time he gives this freedom, this not only elevates the individual soul, but adds to his joy for his creations.

Go in joy.

We are here at your side always. When we feel that you have questions, we try to put the answers in your heart and mind. These answers aren't always what you want to hear, so you block them and think that we have not answered you. We always answer with knowledge in a way that will not only give you answers, but will help you learn. Life is a school, and each day is a learning experience. Your free will can override the lessons, but they will be offered to you. At the end of the day, take an inventory of what lessons were offered, how they were offered, and how they were accepted. In this way, you can see if lessons that are offered are repeated often. If so, then there is a needed reason for this. They will be offered until you decide that you have learned this lesson and are ready to move on. You know in your own life that forgiveness was offered to you many times before you accepted that you had acquired the freedom to forgive and go forward. This is a learning tool that will increase your knowledge and understanding.

Go learn and teach

We are here. When your mind is focused, your writing flows like water; when your today interferes it flows like honey. It still flows and is sweet, but much slower. We have lessons to teach to all and messages that need to be heard. The teaching of this listening time is important. When someone reads the truths you have written, they are skeptical that they can hear these truths. All will hear and do hear, but few trust enough to put these thoughts on paper. Teach that these thoughts will never harm or hurt them. The truths that they hear are whispered for the good of their soul. When these truths are written, they can be viewed again and shared again with others. This listening is easy; however, the writing is the hard part. Have them quiet their mind and start with one word, then one sentence.

Go and teach with love and understanding.

We are here and hear your thoughts. You have asked the question as to why God lets bad things happen to good people. God allows each of us to have free will. Our lives are mapped out in a broad sense as to what we want to achieve in this lifetime. We are also allowed to have the choice as to how we achieve those goals. When other souls interact with us, the way we achieve them may change. We may be given different opportunities and different circumstances to be able to achieve those same goals. If our goal in this life is to learn compassion, someone may come one into our life that needs our compassion, but rejects it when we offer it. The timing may be wrong. However, in the rejection, we may learn perseverance and achieve another of our goals. God doesn't rule, he guides as a great teacher would give you guides to learn from. The lessons that we take from this will vary. Do not be dismayed because bad things happen. Those that you perceive as bad for one may not be bad for all. Learning of life's lessons takes many forms. Remember to keep your eyes on the big picture and do not dwell on the small things that distract from your ultimate goal of being one with God. The only way for someone to learn life's true lesson is by living each day with this ultimate goal. Ask each day if today you have advanced along that road toward your ultimate destination.

Go in peace and learn to love.

We are here. The time is good for you to focus on the "hearing." Hearing the direction of the minds that have gone before. We are the culmination of all that is before and all that is after, all knowledge that ever was and all knowledge that ever will be. The reason that we cannot give all to you is that you could not begin to understand all within the realm of your limited experience of this lifetime. Some of the more learned have been given larger amounts and people have been mystified with "their" knowledge. However, it was not just their knowledge. They were given a slice of the whole cosmic pie, but only a tiny slice. The knowledge that is the realm is like a large ocean. The knowledge of one individual on your realm is a thimbleful. Do not be dismayed when you feel inadequate. All are inadequate in the grand scheme. Only God knows all and holds all knowledge.

Go in understanding.

We are here. Listen to us, not your own thoughts. Do not try to put thoughts or ideas into the conscience of the world. Let us come through freely. Do not give us a structure to stay in. We will give you the thoughts and ideas at the time they are needed—and when you are ready to receive them.

We are here by your side. We know the difficulties that you face in order to teach truths. If it was easy, anybody could do it. You have been granted an honor and a duty to spread truths and to tell of God's love for mankind. As a true father loves a child, God loves each of his creations, because he truly created each of you. You are a part, just as a child is part of his father. The part that is of God is the soul of man. The body is a hull created by the thoughts and ideas of man. This is the body clothes that are needed in your realm. They are changed as clothes are changed for the time and the place. The soul remains the same in all lifetimes. The body remembers small portions of the previous lifetimes, but doesn't have soul remembrances. There is too much old trouble and hurts that to carry this forward would weigh down the present lifetime. This soul conscience carries forward and is part of the universal conscience that you have tapped into. Each one contributes to this large body. When you elevate and learn, it enhances this whole.

Go in knowledge and add to your knowledge.

We are here, the time is good. Quiet your heart and mind. The times of your troubled world are still in flux. Your destiny and the destiny of the world as you know it is held in the hands of people who are not worried about their eternal soul, but about the needs of their todays. This is troubling for each of you. Therefore, each of you must center and focus on yourself and your eternity. We have told you before that being self-centered is not bad; it means centering on self. If you do not take care of your eternity, no one else will. The needs of each of you are so great that your entire lifetime should be spent on the project. Be the best that you can be, focusing on God and on his works through you. Ask the question "Will this elevate my soul?" for each action or deed that you perform. If you cannot answer yes, then it is a needless action. Why would anyone want to perform actions that would damage their ability to see eternity at the hand of God? Take each step in one direction only. Do not fear those steps. You are walking in the light of God. Step out in faith and do not turn your head or take a different direction. The path is straight and the way is lighted with light from above.

Go in love and light.

We are here.

There are many people that would have us fear them. They bellow loudly like a bull, so that all who hear will have fear. This builds a wall around them that keeps others at bay. What they are really saying is stay away for I do not trust my feelings and emotions. I do not want to face the issues. This way, no one expresses their true feelings to them. They can stand on their pedestal, confident that their right will prevail.

Those who speak loudest have the least to say. These bellowing ones are not to be feared but pitied because their fears are what we hear in their harsh words.

Go in peace.

We are here, one with you. Be at peace and hold space in your heart. The world or part of your world is in turmoil at this time. It has always been so. Souls grow from adversity and turmoil in times of peace and quiet, but the opportunity for growth is not as great. It is great for those who are oppressed to learn the lessons of love and forgiveness. And it is great for those who are there to help the oppressed to learn the lessons of love and to learn how to give wholeheartedly to those in need. Those who created the oppression are evil and will have to learn the compassion lesson in another time and place. Always remember that things happen just as they are supposed to. Nothing is unexplained in the great plan.

Go in love and peace and pray for those who know no peace.

We are here in your heart and mind.

Do not be afraid of the future, not this month, year, or decade. We are always here. God doesn't take vacations. He is with you always. Quiet your mind and hear us. The problems that you are listening to are nothing but people trying to increase fear in the world. They will say they know the answers to those fears. Then, they will control and help you. They lie. Help yourself with knowledge and prayers for the world. Don't be afraid. What will happen will happen. You can't stop it, but you can stop the way you react to it. You have many angels protecting the people of the planet. Be at peace and pray for peace.

Go in peace and the light of God

We are here and this is a good time to focus on the important issues. You have been thinking a lot lately about focus. Your focus at this time should be in the future, not in the now. Most of the world is so shortsighted. They can only see the near, not the far. How much of a hindrance that is. When your main focus is in years and then even that focus is clouded with the mundane every-day trivia, the range of sight is even less. Clear your vision, clean the lens of your today, and turn your sight on eternity. Only then will your steps be focused in the right direction. Step out in faith that the pathway will lead to eternity, and if you should falter, there will be many hands to guide you who have walked the same pathway. The path will not always be straight and there will be boulders in your way and dust will clog your eyes, but the journey is worth the difficult trek. Step out and be rewarded.

Go in peace and love.

We are here and the time is good to concentrate on your future. We know that you are contemplating what your future will hold. The time on your plain is so short that your future is the time of eyeblinks. Make the most of that time by teaching love and by showing love for your fellowman. Concentrate on the future that your eternity holds. You have gained much, but have far to go. You mind skitters between the now, the then, and the what will be. Just live each moment as if there will be no other. This does not mean stay in the now. Just do and learn as much about love, life, and the elevation of your soul as you can. We realize that the every day intrudes into your path, but clear the intruding vines and keep your walk straight with your eyes on the ultimate goal.

You have questioned again the place which you have named heaven. Do not search for a physical place as you have pictured it. The place in which all reside is not physical, but mental. That is why it is different for each of us. It is what you want it to be. You will be with those that you desire to be with, doing what you desire to do. You do not need a physical body to learn or to heal. The things that are accomplished on our/your plain are accomplished with the mind. When some say they have seen entities meeting them at the moment of near-death, it is because this is what they are comfortable with. After time, that need for a physical body to comfort them changes. We are not just energy either, we are souls. Our body is that of a great mind, just without the holder that is your body.

Be at peace and live in joy.

We are here as always. We have always been with you. We are always with each soul on their journey. We are the universe and then some. How could we not be with each of you? Only those who choose to listen will hear. You are not unique, just open. The thoughts that we project are unique because each individual's need to hear and know is unique, but the truths are always the same. The times are different, but the truth of time immortal is the same. Nothing has ever truly changed, only the setting for those truths. No matter what world, ancient or current, no matter what language or what animal was living at the time. The truths were the same. The souls were put in that time and place to elevate themselves. That is and was the truth. If that was not happening, then they ceased to exist. It is that simple and that complex. If they did not learn the lessons, there was no more school. That is why it is so important in this time and in this place that the lessons should be learned.

Go in peace and learn.

We are here, one with you. Be at peace and hold space in your heart. The world, or part of your world, is in turmoil at this time. It has always been so. Souls grow from adversity and turmoil, but in times of peace and quiet, the opportunity for growth is not as great. It is great for those who are oppressed to learn the lessons of love and forgiveness. And it is great for those who are there to help the oppressed learn the lessons of love and learn how to give wholeheartedly to those in need. Those who created the oppression are evil and will have to learn the compassion lesson another time and place. Always remember that things happen just as they are supposed to. Nothing is unexplained in the great plan.

Go in love and peace and pray for those who know no peace.

We are here in love and with truth. We know that the times you are going through in your personal life are trying. You must keep the important things in the forefront. Keep your eyes on the goal of becoming a better more enlightened person. Elevate yourself to the very highest that you can. Become the person that you were put in this realm to be. Teach peace and help others reach their goals. In helping others, you are elevating yourself. Do not get bogged down in the every-day troubles of the day. Erase the unimportant from the board of your life so that the highlights remain. You will be a more enlightened soul at the end of this life. You will go on to a higher plain and come closer to the Master. You can only do this by focusing your energy on this goal.

Go in love and focus.

We are here and by now you know this with absolute certainty. We are here to guide you, to let you know when to slow down your mind, to remind you of the truths that you might have forgotten, to help you teach other people the truths we have taught you, and to love you and remind you to love and teach each of those that you come in contact with spiritually. Make sure that they are open to the truth and that they realize that the writing comes from the spiritual conscience of all who have gone before. We will be there for anyone who listens with an open heart and mind. My God is the God of eternity, past, present, and forever. When we say *we are here*, that includes all those who God has chosen to guide and direct our writings and teaching. God's hand is in each truth.

Go in love and peace and heal all you touch.

We are here and we recognize that your mind has been on worldly immediate matters. We know that you know the importance of the tomorrow and forever things. The reason and lesson for our message today is the growth of the soul. This growth is the same as a child. The beginning soul was formed by a thought or breath from God. This soul was unknowing and began as a blank page with no writing. As each lesson is learned, the soul advances and the pages become full. Each soul becomes more perfected and closer to the godlike image. New souls are formed and perfected souls are elevated constantly. All souls that have been and ever will be go through this process. Those who are on the earth plain at this time consist of both. Each of you has been in touch with those who seem to be on a higher plain, who have an inner peace. Also, each of you has known the ones who do not seem to understand the basic concepts of souls and eternity. They live in the now with no worry or concern for their soul's future. Most of these are newly formed souls and have many roads to travel. The travel can be hastened with learning. This is the reason for all messages and all knowledge that is imparted to you and others. This knowledge is not only for the elevation of your soul, but for the enlightenment of others.

Go forth and teach the life lessons.

We are here. You can hear us plainly now. We know that you are tired in your body and in your soul. You need to rest both and put both in God's hands. He knows your needs and wants better for you than you do. Make sure to make prayer a part of every day. Thank him for your blessings and ask for guidance. You have had a great weight lifted from you. It was a very hard learning experience. You gained much from it toward your eternal goal. You could have been bitter, but instead became a better person because of it. You have grown so much this past year that you will not have to repeat the lesson of humility ever again. You are learning patience and understanding. Take the time to work making peace with the inner you. This is something that has been very hard for you. You fight your inner voice. Listen to this small sound and you will be a much happier soul.

Live in love.

"We are here and the time is good for you to quiet your hectic thoughts and center on the importance of learning. The more knowledge you have, the more you can impart. The events are ever-changing. Evil and evil deeds are being thwarted every day. Do not let down. Watch and listen for this evil. The days of watchfulness will never cease. The world is in flux, changing daily. God is ever-watchful for the change in the hearts of men. The times are ripe for this universal change. Please understand that this change is not about your nation, even though that is your focus. The event that began this change may have happened here, but the world is watching and must change in every spot where man inhabits that land. The change has to be universal in order to preserve the world as you know it. Otherwise, there is no purpose for this world. If there is no opportunity for soul growth, then he will not plant the harvest. The betterment of eternity for the souls of the future is the primary reason for the creation of this environment. If that purpose is no longer fulfillable, then the need goes away and the place goes away. If the souls that choose to inhabit this place see no potential for betterment, they have no choice. This is a hard lesson for everyone to grasp. However, the results are worthwhile for the future generations.

Go in peace and remain vigilant and understanding.

We are here as always.

Do not fear; however, do prepare. Not with food and drink, but prepare your soul. Would you not want to meet the "most important" person in your lifetime with clean hands? Then, why would you not want to meet your God with a clean soul? Pray often and tell those around you to prepare with prayers of love and peace.

Go in love.

We are here, of course. You never have to doubt our nearness. Step out in faith that everything will be provided to you. Your hard work will pay off. Listen to our wisdom. You are blessed with a hearing that few have. You hear the wisdom of the ages. We would not give you this hearing if we did not want you to heed the speech.

Be at peace.

We are here. Your prayers are always heard. When you pray, this is like an instant messenger that help is needed or that you are troubled. When we are summoned, we are always able to give assistance. You may not be open to receiving the thoughts that we are passing on or may not want to hear the advice that is offered. You would rather interject your own. This only leads to further hurt and trouble. When you pray, pray knowing that you will receive an answer to that prayer or plea. We always answer.

Go in peace and pray.

We are here in your troubled mind. When you only know that God will provide, all things will be given to you. It is very hard for you to let go and not try to control everything and everyone. God will provide for your needs and those of your loved ones.

Of course, we are here in your heart, mind, and soul. Trusting God is hard, and you need to be reminded constantly that he will provide. You saw that this weekend. Remember that throughout this week and throughout your lifetime. The things that God provides may not be those that you have imagined that you want, but those that you need. Money is foremost on your mind at this time. Be a good steward with what you are being given, and the money that you have will always be enough for your needs. Remember that God feed many with little and that he will also feed you. Trust that this will be done.

Go in peace and trust.

We are here. You have been so blessed with your husband to stand by your side, not only in this life, but in many lives. Give thanks to God for this union. We know that you question all of the relationships that you have had. Each was given to you for a reason, a reason to learn what you did not want in a partner. This is the last time you will have this kind of learning experience, so appreciate this and have patience, which you must learn. No one is perfect except the Almighty, so you or anyone on earth and even those who have crossed over know that. That is what heaven is for. You learn and then the next time you come back, you are wiser and have learned much. You learn until you have no need to come back.

Is there only one heaven and one earth? There are many places to learn. However, there is only one Almighty, the One that gives you the choice to learn and stay. Heaven is many places to many different kinds of individual entities, but all are learning places for each one. Some may come back many times in many different forms, but all have to learn lessons based on their knowledge of good and evil. Each has to learn how to learn, to give of themselves, to better their kind. And each has to believe that there is only One who knows all and sees all. No matter their shape or form, right is right, and evil is never right. The outside of these may look different, but on a soul level, they are the same. Do good, get rewarded. Do evil, and go back and learn good.

The One knows all about all; he cannot be deceived. Those you choose to think they can hide their evil are wrong. Nothing is ever hidden from God.

Go in peace and love and do good.

We are here in your heart and mind. You are doing your heart and soul work by healing. You have known that you could do this, but would not surrender and do it. You know that some machines can do this; however, machines don't have a heart that is filled with compassion. That is what only you have. Do not think that you will become rich doing this. The richness will come in your soul, not the money. Do whatever feels right. We will guide you. It is not right to take drugs to heal. Only the things with energy will heal you. Food, plants, and people have this energy. This is the correct way. The machine that you are making has energy, but it is coming from the earth. It can heal, but add your feelings from your heart and it will double the healing. Some people will not accept this. Some will not. Or an operation doesn't heal, it just puts a Band-Aid on a problem. Sometimes this causes more pain than just healing what is broken.

You will be correct in your healing if you will listen to your intuition and pray.

We are surrounding you in love. All the universe wants is healing. There are many ways, but they all start with your love of mankind. Pray each day that you have the love and light to go forward with your inner healing, then you can heal others.

Be blessed each day. You are a child of God. Do his work.

We are here in your mind and soul. Do not be afraid of the future, but be afraid of not doing the spirit work today. Take the time to practice holiness. Do good and help your fellow man. Then, you will have an afterlife not filled with regrets and sorrows about what you should have done. Love those that are close to you and spread that love to all you touch. We know that fear freezes the good deeds that you can do. Do not be afraid of trying to heal. You are not the one who decides to heal someone. God is!

Go in peace in the light of love and walk with God each day.

We are here as always. The sharing has begun. You have to start with one. The next telling of our story will be easier. The lessons we are imparting are so important for your world to hear that you mustn't be afraid of the way you are perceived, but only the way the message is perceived. This is a time of division in your world, the division of good and evil. Those that are doing evil are doing it in the name of their god. They are saying this with their mouth, but are not saying it with their heart. In that place, they know that the destruction is not of their god. However, the destruction is truly of your God. A loving God that wants his people to realize that in order to have a blissful eternity, they must focus on it now. The light that shines in each of you needs nurturing. The way to bliss is through this light. Light stands for goodness. You know that white light when broken down is made of many colors. As this is so, know that the light that shines in each of you is many-faceted also. There is the light of love for mankind, the light of compassion, the light of knowledge, and the light of generosity. All of these and many more together make up your inner light. You can only shine in heaven when all facets are polished on earth. Do not fail in any area. Remember also that you are polished by the rough cloth of adversity. An easy life without trials does nothing to elevate your soul.

Go in the light of love.

We are here and our thoughts hold you close. The message today is one of vigilance. The world that you live in is becoming complacent about the evil ones. Some have been stopped, but many are still doing evil. Your prayers are heard and appreciated. However, many in your world believe they are safe and without a need to fear. That is not so. Join together in a prayer for understanding and join together to become the best and highest you can be. Create an atmosphere of love and understanding so that you may all grow. As weeds choke out flowers, so evil chokes out the ability to do good and hinders the soul's growth. Look first to your own heart and destroy any weeds of hate. Then, begin your own circle, destroying hate and evil by choking it with love and understanding.

Go in peace and love.

We are here and by now you know this with absolute certainty. We are here to guide you, to let you know when to slow down your mind, to remind you of the truths that you might have forgotten, to help you teach other people the truths we have taught you, and to love you and remind you to love and teach each of those that you come in contact with spiritually. Make sure that they are open to the truth and that they realize that the writing comes from the spiritual conscience of all who have gone before. We will be there for anyone who listens with an open heart and mind. My God is the God of eternity, past, present, and forever. When we say *we are here*, that includes all those who God has chosen to guide and direct our writings and teaching. God's hand is in each truth.

Go in love and peace and heal all you touch.

We are here, of course, in the house of the Lord. Just because the people are not acting as God would doesn't mean that he is not close to this place. If our entire purpose on earth is to become closer to God, what better place to learn this than in his house. If we had to learn, then he would have nothing to teach. He teaches love, forgiveness, and compassion. You are a student too. Do not be dismayed by other people's dismissal of this. They are learned, and each student starts in grade 1. Some may have advanced, but are put back a grade when the lessons do not stick with them. They will learn them eventually. If not in this life, maybe in the next or next. The only way to get closer to God is be godlike in your actions, reactions, and deeds. Let your mind be at peace and your mind open to all the love that flows around you each day.

Go in peace and feel loved.

We are here, and do not be afraid of "end times." There is no such thing as the end. Even if you die, that is not the end of your soul. So why would you worry about everyone saying you are in the end of times? Does it mean that it is the time to see God and have him see you? You already do that. The end times will mean the end of evil and all the bad. Does that sound like something you should dread? No, it will be a time of rejoicing, a jubilee or a time of happiness.

You will be with those who crossed over, all those that have died for you, and those that you have been with in many past lives.

Go in peace and do not fear the future.

We are here as always. Do not worry that you have not written lately.

We have been listening to your thoughts and guiding you. We will always be with you.

Do not worry your mind about the state of your country and your world.
You can put your mind at ease. Your world may change in some ways, but it will not be destroyed. There are more good people on this small green ball than there are bad ones.

Many angels are protecting your planet. You can call them what you will—guides, angels, God, or those from different dimensions. They will all see that your world will survive and thrive.

You and your world are very special to us.

We are proud that you want to help other people. In just your caring, you are helping. When you decide when and how often to do this, you will be helped and shown the how to.

For now, just trust that when you see, you do. You see the need someone has and you feel it and you try to do what is needed. For now, that is enough.

Go in love and give this love to all.

Fear is God's caution light. It tells us to proceed with caution. It tells us to examine the fear and ask why. We are afraid of the things that harm us, be it animals, people, or emotions. Fear can be constructive if it changes your path from one of harm into a better one of enlightenment. Do not try to erase the fears. Hiding from them will only make them grow into a many-headed monster. Examine and then decide. The knowing that we feel inside when we fear is truly energy. Someone or something is disrupting our energy flow. Fear should never be ignored, but embraced and examined. There are many people that would have us fear them. Stand up and face these fears with strength. Know that God is beside you and will protect you.

Go in peace and know that you are protected.

We are here and we have heard your quiet thoughts and concerns over the state of your world. We tell you to be at peace; however, that is an impossible task. We will tell you that God's eyes are watching over the universe, not just our tiny place. He has a plan that will not be revealed until the end of time. Until then, stay at peace in your heart that he holds all life as precious, and that when you ask for peace in your heart, it is already given. Push out the negative and stay focused on the good in you and everyone you touch.

Be at peace and go in God's light of love.

We are here. Do not be disturbed by the events of the world. Center your own world. Learn to love without regard for color or creed. Learn to give freely of yourself. When these things are done, your world will be a better place. The war of people against other people in the name of religion is a farce. There is one God. How can there be wars fought about how we get to that God? There is only one path. The concept is so simple that it is hard for most. Fight because you want to fight. Fight for the freedom to believe what you want or go where you want. That will be a fair fight. Fight to stop someone or something from hurting you or your loved ones. That is a good fight. But never fight to say someone's belief in the road to God is wrong.

Go in love and be at peace.

We are here to give you the ageless advice of the collective consciousness. Do not worry about your spelling, worry about your hearing. The truths are the important part. You have made the decision to let many people know the truths. These were not given to you for you to hold. These were given to you to be scattered like seeds in the wind. They will then be seen like being seen by those who are hungry for the truth. In today's world, it is hard to find the real truth. People shout "This is the truth," but are rarely sharing it. Listen to the truth of the heavens and then you will know the real truth.

People are also fearful of the pandemic that is happening now. This was made by man and will be cured by man. One group that wanted fewer people on earth started this plague. They brought sickness and death, but without meaning to, they brought a coming together of the world.

The saying "This too will pass" is true. We don't know a time or date, but it will last less than the wars that we have seen in last twenty years. So do what you can to stay safe and pray for a timely ending.

We are here in your heart. There are people meditating together for an end to the illness that is taking over your planet. This is the only and best medicine to cure not only the illness, but the hate and division that is engulfing your world. When two or more are gathered in my name, there is strength that is sent to high places. Nothing ever happens without a reason. The reason for this is hate and greed. The country you live in is ruled by someone that sees it as a plaything to be pulled apart. The head of your country is a godly man; however, he is surrounded by those that are not truthful with him and not truthful to him. Pray that God will whisper the truth to him.

Go in prayer and enlighten all you touch.

We are here to assure your souls that your lives do not come to a screeching halt when you die. Dying is just a beginning of a blissful adventure. You will be guided by those who you have known before. They will take you to a place of great peace and beauty. You will review your life—all your happy times and trying times. You will have a peaceful place to rest as long as you need to. That may be years or eons. When you are ready, learning opportunities will be given for you to learn. All subjects from A to Z are available to you. What you missed in this life, you can have in this heavenly realm.

This heaven is a paradise of your own making. When you are indeed ready, you will either stay in this paradise and become an advanced soul, or if you have a need to learn lessons by going back to atone or gain painful knowledge in another lifetime, that will be chosen for you. Many souls have had many lifetimes. It is up to you to make the one you are living now one of peace and understanding and love for your fellow man.

Go in understanding of the truths.

We are here and pleased that you have chosen to let the world hear your voice. The people need to know truths and feel peace that comes with those truths. There are false prophets that shout that they know when the end-times are going to come. I am the only one who rules this realm and I am the one who decides when or if there will be an end of time on your world. This may never happen if you come together in peace and understanding of not only this country but this galaxy. There are more souls than you know about. These souls will also influence the possibility of an end of this world.

Go in peace and gain the knowledge of a peaceful planet.

We are here. We rejoice that there are some people in this world that have peace and a nice place to live and enough to be happy and content. This is not a gift that has been given without hard work in this life and many lives. Do not feel guilty if this is you. Just thank God and pass this on by giving, not always money, but love and understanding to each one you touch. Money does not make happiness; however, friendship or kindness "means a million."

Do not think that we are not at war. We are at war. A war against the good being done by our president. A war against the new technology that is going to change our world. A war against the new tolerance of gender, race, and religion that is uniting our country. We are still at war for the truth that has been withheld from us for way too long. A war against those who want to deny that our world is not this little blue marble, but galaxies and races too numerous to count.

Go in the knowledge that truth will prevail.

We are here to advise you on how to become one. One with God and all his followers. One with those who may not think or vote or live as we do. One with the downtrodden and those who have had the happiness taken from them.

Can we take one minute or one day or one month of our time to join with them? Then, we might understand that they could just as easily have been us.

Go in peace and understanding of your fellow man.

We are here and have vowed to help you in this crisis and any future ones. Your mind is like your body. If you keep it fed and clear out the things that are bad for use, you will stay alert and healthy. However, if you allow your mind to be filled with garbage (untruths), unclean thoughts or actions, greed, or hate, then it will not function as it should and you will become sick in body and soul.

We are here in your heart and mind. You have questioned ascension.

Ascension is going higher. We can ascend into heaven when we die. We can also ascend into a higher level of consciousness, which means we go to a higher level of knowledge and understanding while remaining in this plain. Both of these meanings are positive. We strive for the latter and believe that we will be blessed by the former.

Go in harmony and enlightenment.

We are here. We always hear and advise even if you don't write. We know that this has been a very busy and upsetting time. Try to quiet your mind and soul. God is always and always will be here. We, his messengers, are always here too. We are part of the universal consciousness, but always controlled and enlightened by the father God. It has been said that this is a year of disclosure. We feel that that will be somewhat true. All things will be brought to light.

All beings, no matter the size, color, or dwelling, have a conscience and everyone is part of that conscience. Some put blocks on themselves to keep others out of that knowing. The blocks can be evil acts or minds that stay closed from the goodness. This is sad for those that practice this closed-off mind. They stay in the dark instead of the light of God's grace. If they could understand that, his light would erase the darkness in their lives. This has always been so and will always be so for some. Others will begin to let the light shine and accept and let in the good, rather than turning away.

Your mind has asked your husband. He is one that at one time knew the light and was practicing the way of goodness. However, he turned away and this caused so much hurt in so many. He has much to atone for. He has a chance to learn in the peace and quiet of this realm. However, the test will be in his next life. He will have many trials and problems to overcome. He will never be able to feel the love he had in the life he just left.

Go in peace and forgive, not for the one you forgive but for yourself. Do not hold on to the bitterness or it will make you bitter.

We are here. You have been asked many times about the mechanics of what you do. Those who truly want to have the truths have to listen. Listen not with your ears, but with your heart and mind. Quieten the clutter of your mind and your world first. Pray that anything that comes through is of good and of God. If you do not believe that, abandon it until you have prayed and quietened your mind again. Then listen again. If it is not meant for you to hear these messages, you won't.

There are other things that are enlightening. You can read and listen to those that have been given this gift—when you tear this fiber, it destroys that bond. The ability to help is gone. The chain has been broken. The illness will go away; however, the bonds may not be reforged. Look to the maker to heal these wounds. Stay open to your family, friends, and neighbors. They are feeling this same loss. Do not let evil put a wedge between any.

Go in peace and practice love.

We are here, do not fear. Fear is a brick that closes the door to freedom, not only of thought but of love. Love your fellow man and the freedom to pursue the goals you have set. We are all put on this earth to attain goals that were molded in heaven. When we don't achieve these, we must repeat a lifetime in which we will achieve them.

Go in peace and release fear.

We are here. Do not try to force messages that we want you to write. This will give many a chance to hear the truth that they have forgotten because they are always around us. However, there are times that we choose not to hear. That way, we don't have to hear the knowledge. We can turn away and do our own thing. That thing or things may be following false prophets that will lead into and on to roads of destruction—destruction of their beliefs and their knowing . . . the knowing that there is one God and he is the only one who imparts all truth.

We are here. God has many facets. He is a lover of all mankind. He is a teacher of all truths. He is a patient father to anyone who wants to hold his hand and walk with him. He is a scribe who writes on the slate of knowing the truths that have been there since time began. He is a seer of the beauty and majesty of his creation. He makes no distinction between any of his children as they are perfect in his sight. That doesn't mean that he does not chastise those who know right but commit wrong.

Go in peace and love. – Dad

We are here in your heart and hand. Your love of all is admirable. This is a hard attribute to attain. Some have a hard time giving love with open hands. We clutch our possessions and cherish things instead of people. Each time you give of yourself, you elevate your soul. If people only knew the wealth that they can store up in heaven, they would look at things differently. We know that you have several "treasure boxes" that you share with your grandchildren. Do not forget to also share the treasures that mean most—the love of God and mankind.

Go in love.

We are here. The most important thing that you need to learn today is that everything happens for a reason. Sometimes, it is karma. Things that happen in a past life can be atoned in one or many lives. Sometimes, these are bad or misguided things or sometimes deeds against others that are hurtful. This can be a wonderful, fulfilling lifetime with karmic debt paid. However, it can be a troubling lifetime filled with boulders in your path. Either way, you will grow and learn.

We are here in the time of much turmoil. Everyone is worried about the illness. This keeps them centered on self. Those few who have changed that focus to others are the true heroes of this time. Not only is your nation changing, so is your world. This year was called the year of disclosure. We have seen many disclosures in the world and beyond. This had to happen in order for the cosmos to band together for the greater good.

Not everything unseen is evil. God holds all in his hands. Do not be afraid of the unknown. What we know, we will not fear. It is like a small child in a dark room who thinks there are monsters under the bed. In the daylight, he will realize they are just his toys. Our discovery of these things we did not understand will throw a light on the universe. These things that were not told will be shown soon.

We are here. We know the sadness you have for the illness that is affecting your world. This has been called a cleansing by some, or an earth change by many. It is neither. It is a scourge from an evil source. It is meant to decrease the population. This is something that has been planned for centuries. Decrease in order to control is and has been the plan. This did not start on your earth only. However, the plan has worked. Not only do you have the illness to deal with, but also the distancing from each other. That has been an integral part of your world. The family prays together and stays together.

We are here to advise you of the truths. The first and greatest thing that you need to know is God sees foresees everything. He knows the past, present, and future of all. The present has a reason for happening, whether that is war or peace, great happiness or great sorrow. Things happen for a reason and a purpose. God is all good. He would never destroy just to destroy. His purpose is always for the better good. It may be to remind those affected to pray and work toward peace. It may be a cleansing of evil to be replaced by good. It may also be to bring those affected closer to him. He created heaven and all things in this universe and others. If his creations are drifting off course, the course that he mapped out for them, then he will change that course. That may be for a short period; however, it can be for an eternity. As long as we keep our eyes on him and remember our life purpose, then we can rejoice in a fruitful journey. He leaves the decision of our destiny on each of us.

Keep the love of God in your life.

Who are we? And how do we think we are so great that we can give advice to you? We are the cosmic consciousness which starts with God and includes those he has chosen to be guides, guardians, disciples, and knowers of the eternal truths.

We are here in your thoughts of giving your knowledge of truths to all who need to hear. God was and is eternal. He was the beginning and is never ending. When he guides you in your writing, it is with the hope that you will feel his presence and heed his guidance. Because he has gifted you with free will, you can turn your eyes away from him.

However, this departure can lead to deep despair, like a young child who gets lost and wanders away and searches for his parents to lead him home.

When we are lost and do not see that path to God, we search for someone to lead us. However, if we choose the wrong hand to guide us, it can lead us to a path that causes pain and self-destruction. Then, you will have to travel over many boulders and face many great mountains in order to get back on that path. Make sure to follow the leader that has been led by God to hold your hand and be your guide.